15Minute.Fitness Family Friendly Meals

Jackie Schwartz

&

Jonas Schwartz

Copyright © 2021 Jackie Schwartz

All rights reserved.

ISBN: 978-1-7366864-2-3

DEDICATION

This book is dedicated to our clients. When you came to us to lose weight, we asked you to trust us and trust the process. You did, and now you have healthier bodies and healthier families. Nothing makes us happier. We are so excited to be able to spread that health to others. Thank you for having faith in us.

ACKNOWLEDGMENTS

I would like to sincerely thank all of our clients. This book would not be possible without them. It is a collection of meals that we have shared with each other to support each other. Now these same meals will support others. Nothing makes us happier than creating healthy lives and families.

15Minute.Fitness Family Friendly Meals

www.15minute.fitness

Table Of Contents

Breakfast

Egg Bake Casserole	4
Crustless Broccoli Ham Quiche	6
Jonas's PBJ	8
Jonas's Egg Sandwich	10
Jonas's French Toast	12

Sides and Salads

Broccoli Cauliflower Salad	16
Asian Zoodle Salad	18
Noodle Salad	20

Meals and Casseroles

Sausage Bake	24
Shrimp and Sausage Stir Fry	26
Turkey Beer Chili	28
Mexican Stir Fry	30
Pizza Chaffle	32
Chicken and Spinach Quesadillas	34
Keto Chicken Casserole	36
Mexican lasagna	38
Homemade Sloppy Joes	40
Crustless Skillet Pizza	42
Chicken Zucchini Casserole	44
Chicken Cordon Bleu Casserole	46
Chicken Chili	48
Chicken and Veggie Pan Meal	50

Buffalo Chicken Casserole	52
Beef and Veggie Soup	54
Beef and Broccoli Stir Fry	56
Cabbage Stew	58
Cajun Stir Fry	60
Chicken Bacon Ranch Casserole	62
Chicken Verde	64
Chicken Taco Soup	66
Coconut Curry Chicken	68
Creamy Cajun Pasta	70
Eggroll In A Bowl	72
Ginger Honey Pork	74
Italian Zucchini Noodles	76
One Pan Oven Pork Chops	78
Sauerkraut Skillet	80
Zucchini Lasagna	82
Zucchini Tacos	84

Desserts

"Apple" Crisp	88
Pumpkin Bread Pudding	90
Banana Bread	92
Low Fat Cupcakes	94
Protein "Ice Cream"	96

Afterword

	98

FOREWORD

We were tired of pouring through recipe books, trying to find a new meal to prepare from time to time—only to find a recipe that looked good…but failed to meet ANY kind of standards in terms of nutrition and health. Our Sine-Wave diet is flexible, but it is much easier to accommodate an occasional splurge than to blindly accept daily meals that totally "blow the bank" in terms of calories or macronutrients.

So, we determined to compile a book full of recipes that FIT into a high protein, low calorie diet model, so we (and our clients) could have a go-to source for new meal ideas.

However, in line with our principles at 15Minute.Fitness, these recipes had other criteria in order to merit inclusion here. Not only did they have to fit into a reasonable diet model, they had to be quick. We can't prescribe 15 minute workouts and then ask you to trade the hours you save in the gym for hours slaving over a hot stove. That would be dumb!

All these meals should have a prep time of 15 minutes or less. Cook time may vary, but you can do other things (like squeeze in a 15 minute workout!) while your food actually cooks.

Also, our ultimate focus is on transforming families from disease and disorder to a state of health. This means these meals should be amenable to husbands, wives and children. Each of these recipes has been husband, wife AND kid approved. While that may not mean everyone will like every one of the recipes (and it may take more than one exposure to attain permanent approval), every recipe here has found favor with some real families we know.

15Minute.Fitness Family Friendly Meals

We sincerely hope this collection of recipes will help you fit healthy food into the lives of yourself and your family. We pray this finds a place in your kitchen as a resource to make health and fitness just a little bit easier, a little bit more attainable, a little less overwhelming and a lot more REAL in YOUR world.

We love you, and we want to help you and your family live long, healthy, happy lives. You have incredible transformative influence in the lives of the people you love. Let's work together to insure that our power as role

models is used in the best ways possible. While physical fitness and health is only one part of the equation (together with mental, emotional and spiritual health), it is vitally important to every being who has a body. That's you, me and all our loved ones.

Blessings!

15Minute.Fitness Family Friendly Meals

www.15minute.fitness

Healthy Cooking Tips and Tricks

Changing to a healthier way of eating does not mean having to give up everything you love. Nothing is completely off limits in moderation. Remember that it is your weekly average of calories that is important, not your day-to-day count. If you know you will have a big meal on Friday night, then eat a little fewer calories on the day before or after the event.

Many of the recipes in this book do not have any carbs added. If you are counting carbs or calories, you may leave them out as the recipe does. If you are not counting calories (and for your kids), many of the recipes can be served with brown rice, quinoa or other whole grain carbs. On days that we eat lean before a big meal, carbs and fats are the first things we take out.

Almost any recipe can be altered to be healthier. That is what we have done in most of the recipes in this book. Making smart substitutions is the key. Replacing full fat cheese with fat free cheese, sour cream with fat free Greek yogurt, tortillas and bread with lower carb varieties instantly lowers calories. Adding extra vegetables into casseroles, soups and stir frys adds volume without too many extra calories. You can toss a bag of cauliflower rice into almost any crockpot meal, and it will be unnoticeable.

Our most frequently repeated comments are about getting the kids to eat new foods and vegetables. Like weight loss, this can just take time. Kids have to be introduced and taste a new food several times before they become adapted to the taste. I used the three-bite rule with my boys. They had to take three bites before they could say they did not like it. And I did not make different meals for my kids. They learned that mom made one dinner and they had to find something on the plate they liked and would eat. Casseroles are an easy start for a lot of introductions.

You can tell your kids they can pick out what they don't like after three bites. Since flavors blend in casseroles the vegetables end up very flavorful. Remember kids want their food to taste good. So, make vegetables flavorful. If you are not thrilled with plain steamed broccoli, you cannot expect them to be either. Let them add cheese or ranch. It is better for them to eat their vegetables with an unhealthy topping than to not have the vegetables at all. After a while the amount of cheese and ranch will become less as they learn to like their vegetables.

15Minute.F.tness Family Friendly Meals

Breakfast

Egg Bake Casserole

By Jackie Schwartz

Makes 4 Servings

Ingredients

- 4 oz turkey breakfast sausage
- 16 oz canned mushrooms
- 12 oz frozen spinach, squeezed
- 8 large eggs
- 1 cup fat free shredded cheddar cheese
- Salt and pepper to taste

Preparation

1. Cook sausage and cool. Drain mushrooms. Add all ingredients and mix well in a bowl with salt and pepper.
2. Pour into a sprayed baking dish. Bake at 350 for about 30 minutes or until set.

Whole Egg Casserole with Cheese

Nutrition Facts

Serving Size: 1 Serving

Amount Per Serving		% Daily Value*
Calories	309.6 kcal	15 %
Total Fat	13.6 g	21 %
Saturated Fat	4.1 g	20 %
Trans Fat	0 g	
Cholesterol	405.5 mg	135 %
Sodium	978.2 mg	41 %
Total Carbohydrate	14.2 g	5 %
Dietary Fiber	5.5 g	22 %
Sugars	5.2 g	
Protein	33.2 g	66 %

Vitamin A	210 %	Vitamin C	8 %
Calcium	42 %	Iron	24 %

* Percent Daily Values are based on a 2,000 calorie diet. Your daily values may be higher or lower depending on your calorie needs.

Full Info at cronometer.com </>

Crustless Broccoli Ham Quiche

By Christine Maier

Makes 6 Servings

Ingredients

- 3 cups broccoli florets
- 1 cup shredded fat free cheddar cheese
- 8 oz diced ham
- 5 large eggs
- ⅔ cup 2% milk
- 4 tbsp fat free half and half

Preparation

1. Mix eggs with milk and half and half.
2. Add Broccoli, ham and cheese.
3. Pour into casserole dish and bake at 350 for approximately 1 hour or until set.

Crustless Broccoli, Cheese, & Ham Quiche (Christine Maier)

Nutrition Facts

Serving Size: 1 Serving

Amount Per Serving		% Daily Value*
Calories	166 kcal	8 %
Total Fat	6 g	9 %
Saturated Fat	1.9 g	10 %
Trans Fat	0 g	
Cholesterol	178.1 mg	59 %
Sodium	690.9 mg	29 %
Total Carbohydrate	7.7 g	3 %
Dietary Fiber	1.5 g	6 %
Sugars	4.8 g	
Protein	20 g	40 %
Vitamin A	13 % • Vitamin C	0 %
Calcium	26 % • Iron	7 %

* Percent Daily Values are based on a 2,000 calorie diet. Your daily values may be higher or lower depending on your calorie needs.

Full Info at cronometer.com </>

Jonas's PBJ

By Jonas Schwartz

Makes 1 Serving

Ingredients

- 2 sliced Aldi Keto bread
- 4 tbsp powdered peanut butter
- 2 tbsp sugar free jelly

Preparation

1. Mix powdered peanut butter with just enough water to make spreadable use to make a healthy version of a PBJ.

Jonas's PJB

Nutrition Facts

Serving Size: 1 full recipe

Amount Per Serving		% Daily Value*
Calories	200 kcal	10 %
Total Fat	5 g	8 %
Saturated Fat	0 g	0 %
Trans Fat	0 g	
Cholesterol	0 mg	0 %
Sodium	360 mg	15 %
Total Carbohydrate	36 g	12 %
Dietary Fiber	26 g	104 %
Sugars	2 g	
Protein	22 g	44 %
Vitamin A	- % • Vitamin C	- %
Calcium	6 % • Iron	11 %

* Percent Daily Values are based on a 2,000 calorie diet. Your daily values may be higher or lower depending on your calorie needs.

Full Info at cronometer.com </>

Tip

This "recipe" is added to show how simple substitutions can make big differences. A regular peanut butter sandwich on white bread with regular peanut butter and jelly has 485 calories, 16 grams of protein, 59 grams of carbohydrates and 19 grams of fat!

15Minute.Fitness Family Friendly Meals

Jonas's Egg Sandwich

By Jonas Schwartz

Makes 1 Serving

Ingredients

- 1 Aldi Keto bun
- 4 large egg whites
- 1 slice fat free cheese
- 3 pieces thin sliced ham

Preparation

Cook egg whites and assemble into a sandwich - we like to cook our eggs in a microwave egg poacher.

1. Add mustard or FF Greek yogurt if you like.

Jonas's Egg Sandwich		
Nutrition Facts Serving Size: 1 full recipe		
Amount Per Serving		% Daily Value*
Calories	194.5 kcal	10 %
Total Fat	3.5 g	5 %
Saturated Fat	0.5 g	3 %
Trans Fat	0 g	
Cholesterol	17.5 mg	6 %
Sodium	1001.8 mg	42 %
Total Carbohydrate	25.5 g	8 %
Dietary Fiber	19 g	76 %
Sugars	3.4 g	
Protein	32.6 g	65 %
Vitamin A	12 % • Vitamin C	1 %
Calcium	21 % • Iron	8 %
* Percent Daily Values are based on a 2,000 calorie diet. Your daily values may be higher or lower depending on your calorie needs.		
Full Info at cronometer.com		</>

Tip

This "recipe" is added to show how simple substitutions can make big differences.

15Minute.Fitness Family Friendly Meals

Jonas's French Toast

By Jonas Schwartz

Makes 1 Serving

Ingredients

- 4 slices of Aldi Keto Bread
- 1 cup liquid egg whites
- 6 Tbsp sugar free syrup

Preparation

1. Dip Bread into egg whites.
2. Cook on griddle with a spray of Pam.
3. Top with Sugar free syrup or topping of choice!

Jonas's French Toast

Nutrition Facts

Serving Size: 1 full recipe — 396g

Amount Per Serving		% Daily Value*
Calories	310 kcal	16 %
Total Fat	6 g	9 %
Saturated Fat	0 g	0 %
Trans Fat	0 g	
Cholesterol	0 mg	0 %
Sodium	1190 mg	50 %
Total Carbohydrate	60 g	20 %
Dietary Fiber	48 g	192 %
Sugars	0 g	
Protein	46 g	92 %
Vitamin A	- % • Vitamin C	- %
Calcium	9 % • Iron	0 %

* Percent Daily Values are based on a 2,000 calorie diet. Your daily values may be higher or lower depending on your calorie needs.

Full Info at cronometer.com   </>

Tip

You can top this with fresh fruit, sugar free jelly, or a homemade icing from Splenda and Greek yogurt.

Sides and Salads

15Minute.Fitness Family Friendly Meals

Broccoli Cauliflower Salad

By Julie Houston

Makes 12 Servings

Ingredients

- 1 head broccoli, chopped
- 1 head cauliflower, chopped
- ½ lb turkey bacon, cooked and chopped
- 1 cup shredded fat-free cheddar cheese
- 2 cups nonfat plain Greek yogurt
- ½ cup Stevia
- ½ teaspoon salt

Preparation

1. Mix broccoli, cauliflower, bacon, and shredded cheese in a large bowl.
2. In a small bowl, mix Greek yogurt, Stevia, and salt until well blended.
3. Pour yogurt mixture over the vegetable mixture and stir well.
4. Eat immediately or chill until ready to serve.

Broccoli Cauliflower Salad (Julie Houston)

Nutrition Facts

Serving Size	1 Serving

Amount Per Serving

Calories 93.4

		% Daily Value*
Total Fat	1.7 g	2 %
Saturated Fat	0.5 g	3 %
Trans Fat	0 g	
Cholesterol	18.1 mg	6 %
Sodium	370.2 mg	16 %
Total Carbohydrate	8.7 g	3 %
Dietary Fiber	2.6 g	9 %
Total Sugars	3.8 g	
Added Sugars	0 g	0 %
Protein	12.3 g	
Vitamin D	0 mcg	0 %
Calcium	143.4 mg	11 %
Iron	0.8 mg	5 %
Potassium	433.7 mg	9 %

* The % Daily Value (DV) tells you how much a nutrient in a serving of food contributes to a daily diet. 2,000 calories a day is used for general nutrition advice.

Full Info at cronometer.com

15Minute.Fitness Family Friendly Meals

Asian Zoodle Salad

By Jackie Schwartz

Makes 6 Servings

Ingredients

- 4 Zucchini made into noodles
- 1 Red Bell Pepper, chopped
- 1 Small bunch Green Onions, chopped
- ½ cup chopped Cilantro
- 2 tbsp sesame oil
- 6 tbsp seasoned rice vinegar
- ½ tbsp ginger paste
- ½ tbsp garlic paste
- Dash of salt
- Dash of cayenne pepper

Preparation

1. Combine zucchini noodles, chopped red bell pepper, green onions and cilantro in a large bowl.
2. Mix remaining ingredients in a separate bowl with a whisk
3. Top zucchini mix with dressing and let marinate for at least one hour before serving.

Asian Zoodle Salad

Nutrition Facts

Serving Size: 1 Serving

Amount Per Serving		% Daily Value*
Calories	100.8 kcal	5 %
Total Fat	5.2 g	8 %
Saturated Fat	0.8 g	4 %
Trans Fat	0 g	
Cholesterol	0 mg	0 %
Sodium	941 mg	39 %
Total Carbohydrate	12.9 g	4 %
Dietary Fiber	2.2 g	9 %
Sugars	10.9 g	
Protein	2.1 g	4 %
Vitamin A	36 % • Vitamin C	101 %
Calcium	3 % • Iron	4 %

* Percent Daily Values are based on a 2,000 calorie diet. Your daily values may be higher or lower depending on your calorie needs.

Full Info at cronometer.com </>

Noodle Salad

By Jackie Schwartz

Makes 10 Servings

Ingredients

- 8 oz Edamame Spaghetti
- 2 packages Pasta Zero or other Shirataki Spaghetti
- 3 tbsp Accent flavoring
- 3 tbsp lemon juice
- 1 can chopped black olives
- 11 jar pimentos
- 6 stalks celery, chopped
- 1 bell pepper, chopped
- 1 ½ cups fat free Greek yogurt

Preparation

1. Cook edamame spaghetti according to directions on box and drain.
2. Rinse Pasta Zero and add to spaghetti. Add remaining ingredients.
3. Place in the refrigerator for at least 2 hours. It is better overnight.

Noodle Salad

Nutrition Facts

Serving Size: 1 Serving

Amount Per Serving		% Daily Value*
Calories	131.6 kcal	7 %
Total Fat	3.8 g	6 %
Saturated Fat	0.3 g	1 %
Trans Fat	0 g	
Cholesterol	1.8 mg	1 %
Sodium	1344 mg	56 %
Total Carbohydrate	14.3 g	5 %
Dietary Fiber	7.2 g	29 %
Sugars	3.5 g	
Protein	13.8 g	28 %
Vitamin A	3 % • Vitamin C	25 %
Calcium	13 % • Iron	17 %

* Percent Daily Values are based on a 2,000 calorie diet. Your daily values may be higher or lower depending on your calorie needs.

Full Info at cronometer.com </>

Tip

Diced or shredded chicken or ham can be add to be eaten as a cold meal.

Meals and Casseroles

Sausage Bake

By Kathy Petcov

Makes 2 Servings

Ingredients

- Jennie-O Sweet Italian Turkey Sausage
- 12 oz raw mushrooms
- 1 red bell pepper
- 2 green bell peppers
- ½ cup Kraft Fat-Free Mozzarella cheese

Preparation

1. Slice sausage into 1/2 think slices.
2. Slice or Half mushrooms.
3. Cut peppers into 1in squares.
4. Spray casserole dish.
5. Toss above ingredients in casserole dish and lightly salt. Bake at 350 for 20 minutes. Cover with cheese and bake additional 10 minutes.

Sausage Bake (Kathy Petcov)

Nutrition Facts

Serving Size: 1 Serving

Amount Per Serving		% Daily Value*
Calories	348.5 kcal	17 %
Total Fat	13.2 g	20 %
Saturated Fat	4 g	20 %
Trans Fat	0 g	
Cholesterol	115 mg	38 %
Sodium	894.5 mg	37 %
Total Carbohydrate	15.7 g	6 %
Dietary Fiber	5.5 g	22 %
Sugars	3.7 g	
Protein	42.9 g	86 %
Vitamin A	50 % • Vitamin C	295 %
Calcium	27 % • Iron	17 %

* Percent Daily Values are based on a 2,000 calorie diet. Your daily values may be higher or lower depending on your calorie needs.

Full Info at cronometer.com

Shrimp and Sausage Stir Fry

By Lauren Slovak

Makes 4 Servings

Ingredients

- 16 oz raw shrimp
- 6 oz Turkey Smoked Sausage
- 1 Raw Zucchini
- 1 Red bell pepper
- 6 oz fresh mushrooms
- 1 tsp Old Bay seasoning

Preparation

1. Stir fry all ingredients in a large skillet until shrimp and vegetables are cooked.

Shrimp and Sausage Stir Fry (Lauren Slovak)

Nutrition Facts

Serving Size: 1 Serving

Amount Per Serving		% Daily Value*
Calories	231.4 kcal	12 %
Total Fat	6.3 g	10 %
Saturated Fat	1.8 g	9 %
Trans Fat	0.1 g	
Cholesterol	265.7 mg	89 %
Sodium	1710 mg	71 %
Total Carbohydrate	8.7 g	3 %
Dietary Fiber	1.6 g	6 %
Sugars	3.5 g	
Protein	33.9 g	68 %
Vitamin A	20 % • Vitamin C	51 %
Calcium	12 % • Iron	9 %

* Percent Daily Values are based on a 2,000 calorie diet. Your daily values may be higher or lower depending on your calorie needs.

Full Info at cronometer.com </>

Turkey Beer Chili

By Kevin and Amanda Ford

Makes 10 Servings

Ingredients

- ½ medium onion, chopped
- 1 tbsp olive oil
- 48 oz 93% lean ground turkey
- 3 cloves garlic, minced
- 6 tbsp chili powder
- 6 tbsp cumin
- 6 oz tomato paste
- 2 cans kidney beans
- 2 can petite diced tomatoes
- 30 oz chicken broth
- 1 12oz light beer

Preparation

1. Chop onion and sauté in EVOO on high until tender.
2. Add minced garlic & sauté one minute then reduce to med-high heat.
3. Add turkey, chili powder and cumin. Cook until meat is browned.
4. Add tomato paste and stir to coat meat.
5. Add remaining ingredients and bring to a boil. Reduce heat and simmer until ready to serve.
6. Add salt and pepper to taste.

Turkey Beer chili (Ford)

Nutrition Facts

Serving Size: 1 × 2 Cup

Amount Per Serving		% Daily Value*
Calories	355.1 kcal	18 %
Total Fat	12.5 g	19 %
Saturated Fat	3.5 g	17 %
Trans Fat	0 g	
Cholesterol	97.7 mg	33 %
Sodium	828.1 mg	35 %
Total Carbohydrate	25.5 g	9 %
Dietary Fiber	7 g	28 %
Sugars	7.6 g	
Protein	34.8 g	70 %
Vitamin A	44 % • Vitamin C	17 %
Calcium	13 % • Iron	33 %

* Percent Daily Values are based on a 2,000 calorie diet. Your daily values may be higher or lower depending on your calorie needs.

Full Info at cronometer.com

Mexican Stir Fry

By Lindsey Barak

Makes 10 Servings

Ingredients

- 32 oz 97% lean ground beef
- 4 cups canned black beans, drained
- 4 medium summer squash
- 1 packet taco season mix

Preparation

1. Brown ground beef.
2. Add chopped squash to pan and cook until tender
3. Add beans and taco seasoning and mix with a little water to coat.

Mexican Stir Fry (Lindsey Barak)

Nutrition Facts

Serving Size: 1 Serving

Amount Per Serving		% Daily Value*
Calories	268.5 kcal	13 %
Total Fat	4.9 g	8 %
Saturated Fat	2.2 g	11 %
Trans Fat	0.1 g	
Cholesterol	79.9 mg	27 %
Sodium	821.1 mg	34 %
Total Carbohydrate	25.2 g	8 %
Dietary Fiber	8.9 g	36 %
Sugars	3.5 g	
Protein	31.1 g	62 %
Vitamin A	12 % • Vitamin C	24 %
Calcium	11 % • Iron	29 %

* Percent Daily Values are based on a 2,000 calorie diet. Your daily values may be higher or lower depending on your calorie needs.

Full Info at cronometer.com

Serving Tip

Use this stir fry to fill tacos or use to top buddha bowls or salad.

Pizza Chaffle

By Sorcha Blake

Makes 1 Serving
Ingredients
- 1 large egg

- ½ cup fat free shredded mozzarella cheese
- 1 ½ tsp grated parmesan cheese
- 1 tbsp almond flour
- ¼ tsp Italian seasoning
- ½ tsp garlic powder
- ⅛ cup pizza sauce
- ¼ cup fat free shredded mozzarella cheese
- 5 slices turkey pepperoni

Preparation

1. Mix first 6 ingredients together
2. Spray waffle iron and place half of mixture in waffle iron. Cook until light goes off
3. Let cool for 3 minutes and repeat with other half of mixture
4. Once cooled add toppings and cook in oven at 400 for 3-4 minutes to melt cheese.

Pizza Chaffle (Sorcha Blake)

Nutrition Facts

Serving Size: 1 full recipe

Amount Per Serving		% Daily Value*
Calories	312 kcal	16 %
Total Fat	12.3 g	19 %
Saturated Fat	3.1 g	15 %
Trans Fat	0 g	
Cholesterol	193.6 mg	65 %
Sodium	1263.6 mg	53 %
Total Carbohydrate	10.3 g	3 %
Dietary Fiber	1 g	4 %
Sugars	2.2 g	
Protein	40.8 g	82 %
Vitamin A	5 % • Vitamin C	1 %
Calcium	94 % • Iron	9 %

* Percent Daily Values are based on a 2,000 calorie diet. Your daily values may be higher or lower depending on your calorie needs.

Full Info at cronometer.com

Chicken and Spinach Quesadilla

By Kevin and Amanda Ford

Makes 2 Servings

Ingredients
- 4 Ole High Fiber Wraps
- 8 oz fajita chicken thighs
- 1-2 cups raw spinach
- 2 cups fat free shredded cheddar cheese

Preparation
1. Heat griddle to 350° and place all tortillas down to warm. Divide cheese and spread evenly over all tortillas.

2. Allow cheese to partially melt. Layer spinach and chicken on two tortillas, then place the other tortillas on top (cheese side down). Tap the top tortilla with the flat side of a spatula and then flip quesadilla over. Tap again until cheese is completely melted and all ingredients stay in place.

3. Cut into quarters and serve with your favorite sour cream substitute

Chicken & Spinach Quesadillas (Ford)

Nutrition Facts

Serving Size: 1 Serving

Amount Per Serving		% Daily Value*
Calories	423.5 kcal	21 %
Total Fat	11.1 g	17 %
Saturated Fat	2.5 g	13 %
Trans Fat	0 g	
Cholesterol	75 mg	25 %
Sodium	2461.9 mg	103 %
Total Carbohydrate	45.5 g	15 %
Dietary Fiber	22.3 g	89 %
Sugars	0.1 g	
Protein	61.4 g	123 %
Vitamin A	28 % • Vitamin C	7 %
Calcium	121 % • Iron	16 %

* Percent Daily Values are based on a 2,000 calorie diet. Your daily values may be higher or lower depending on your calorie needs.

Full Info at cronometer.com

Keto Chicken Casserole

By Julie Houston

Makes 8 Servings

Ingredients

- 1 tbsp coconut oil
- 1/2 cup red onion, diced
- 6 oz baby bella mushrooms
- 5 oz baby spinach
- 4 oz fat free cream cheese
- 1/2 cup grated parmesan
- 3/4 cup fat-free cheddar cheese
- 3/4 non-fat Greek yogurt
- 2 tsp cornstarch
- 3 cloves garlic, minced
- 1 tsp dijon mustard/dressing
- 1/2 lb turkey bacon, cooked & chopped
- 15 oz cooked chicken
- 1 tsp Italian seasoning
- 1/2 tsp salt
- 1/2 tsp black pepper
- 1/2 cup fat-free shredded mozzarella

Preparation

1. Preheat the oven to 375°F
2. In a small bowl mix the Greek yogurt with the cornstarch until well blended and set aside.
3. Preheat a large skillet to medium high heat and add 1 tbsp coconut oil.
4. Add the onions and mushrooms and saute for 3-5 minutes until tender. Add the spinach and cook for 1-2 minutes until wilted down.
5. Turn the heat down to medium and add in the Greek yogurt, cream cheese, mustard, garlic and cheddar cheese and mix well.
6. Add in the cooked bacon, seasonings and the chicken. Stir to combine.
7. Spray casserole dish with olive oil and transfer the entire skillet contents to dish.
8. Top the casserole with mozzarella cheese and bake for 10-12 minutes. Top with grated parmesan.

Mexican Lasagna

By Kevin and Amanda Ford

Makes 4 Servings

Ingredients

- 16 oz. 93% lean ground turkey
- 2 cups fat free shredded cheddar cheese
- 16 Mr. Tortilla, 1 Carb Tortillas, Multigrain
- 2 cups frozen fajita vegetables
- 2 cups red enchilada sauce
- 1 package Taco Seasoning

Preparation

1. Preheat oven to 375°. Spray 8"×8" casserole dish with non-stick spray.
2. Add raw turkey meat, fajita veggies and taco seasoning to a skillet. Cook on med-high heat until meat is browned and veggies are softened. Divide mixture into four equal sections.
3. Spread about 1/4 cup of sauce on bottom of casserole dish. Place four tortillas over the sauce as the bottom of your first layer. Spread 1/2 cup of sauce over tortillas, then 1/4 of meat mixture, then 1/2 cup of cheese. Repeat until you have four layers total.

Mexican lasagna (Ford)

Nutrition Facts

Serving Size: 1 Serving

Amount Per Serving		% Daily Value*
Calories	377.8 kcal	19 %
Total Fat	10.3 g	16 %
Saturated Fat	2.5 g	13 %
Trans Fat	0 g	
Cholesterol	85 mg	28 %
Sodium	1797.5 mg	75 %
Total Carbohydrate	31.5 g	10 %
Dietary Fiber	9 g	36 %
Sugars	4.3 g	
Protein	45 g	90 %
Vitamin A	18 % • Vitamin C	16 %
Calcium	70 % • Iron	22 %

* Percent Daily Values are based on a 2,000 calorie diet. Your daily values may be higher or lower depending on your calorie needs.

Full Info at cronometer.com

Homemade Sloppy Joes

By Christine Maier

Makes 4 Servings

Ingredients

- 16 oz ground venison (Or very lean ground beef)
- 1 cup ketchup
- 1 tbsp mustard
- 1 tbsp distilled vinegar

Preparation

1. Brown Venison.
2. Add remaining ingredients and stir until combined and heated through.
3. Serve on low carb bread or buns.

Sloppy Joes (Christine Maier)

Nutrition Facts

Serving Size: 1 Serving

Amount Per Serving		% Daily Value*
Calories	237.5 kcal	12 %
Total Fat	7.8 g	12 %
Saturated Fat	3.7 g	19 %
Trans Fat	0.2 g	
Cholesterol	91.1 mg	30 %
Sodium	659.7 mg	27 %
Total Carbohydrate	16.7 g	6 %
Dietary Fiber	0.3 g	1 %
Sugars	12.8 g	
Protein	25.4 g	51 %
Vitamin A	6 % • Vitamin C	4 %
Calcium	2 % • Iron	19 %

* Percent Daily Values are based on a 2,000 calorie diet. Your daily values may be higher or lower depending on your calorie needs.

Full Info at cronometer.com

Crustless Skillet Pizza

By Julie Houston

Makes 8 Servings

Ingredients

- 2 lbs Ground meat, lean
- 1 tsp Basil, dried
- 1 tsp Oregano, dried
- 1/2 cup Red onion
- 1/2 cup Bell pepper
- 1 1/2 cups Pizza sauce
- 1 tsp Black pepper
- 2 tsp Sea salt
- 1 1/2 cup fat free shredded mozzarella cheese
- 1 1/2 cup fat free shredded cheddar cheese

Preparation

1. Preheat oven to 425 degrees Fahrenheit.
2. In a medium-size bowl, combine meat, oregano, basil, salt and pepper together.
3. Spread meat mixture evenly on cast iron skillet, spreading to the walls of the skillet.
4. Bake meat patty for 25 minutes.
5. When meat is cooked, remove from oven. The meat patty should slightly shrink in size. Drain out any grease.
6. Spread pizza sauce directly on top of the meat, making sure to get the outside of the patty.
7. Cover the pizza sauce with 2 cups of cheese, followed by toppings.
8. Top with additional 1 cup of cheese and return to oven for another 15 minutes or until vegetables are tender and cheese is bubbling.
9. Remove from oven and let sit for 10 minutes. Cut slices and enjoy immediately.

Chicken Zucchini Casserole

By Julie Houston

Makes 8 Servings

Ingredients

- 12 oz cooked chicken breast, shredded or chopped
- 8 oz mushrooms, raw
- ½ large onion, chopped
- 3 medium zucchini, chopped or sliced
- ½ cup chicken broth
- ⅔ tbsp cornstarch
- 1 cup fat free Greek yogurt
- ¾ cup fat free shredded mozzarella cheese
- 1 cup fat free shredded mozzarella cheese
- Dash of salt and pepper

Preparation

1. Sauté onions, mushroom and zucchini until tender and set aside in a bowl.
2. Simmer chicken broth with cornstarch until thickened. Remove from heat and stir in yogurt, ¾ cups cheese and salt and pepper.
3. Drain any liquid from vegetables and mix with chicken and cheese sauce.
4. Transfer to a q-quart baking dish and top with remaining cheese.
5. Bake at 400 degrees for 20-25 minutes. Let stand 10 minutes before serving.

Chicken Cordon Bleu Casserole

By Julie Houston

Chicken Cordon Bleu Casserole [Copy]

Nutrition Facts
Serving Size: 1 Serving

Amount Per Serving		% Daily Value*
Calories	185.4 kcal	9 %
Total Fat	5 g	8 %
Saturated Fat	1.2 g	6 %
Trans Fat	0 g	
Cholesterol	77.1 mg	26 %
Sodium	551.3 mg	23 %
Total Carbohydrate	4.5 g	1 %
Dietary Fiber	1 g	4 %
Sugars	2.7 g	
Protein	31.2 g	62 %
Vitamin A	6 % • Vitamin C	47 %
Calcium	20 % • Iron	4 %

* Percent Daily Values are based on a 2,000 calorie diet. Your daily values may be higher or lower depending on your calorie needs.

Full Info at cronometer.com

Makes 12 Servings

Ingredients

- 1 head cauliflower (cut into florets)
- 2 Tbsp olive oil
- Sea salt
- Black pepper
- 1/3 cup non-fat Greek yogurt with 3/4 tsp of corn starch
- 1/2 cup non-fat Greek yogurt
- 2 tbsp Dijon mustard/dressing
- 2 cloves Garlic (minced)
- 1 1/2 lb shredded cooked chicken
- 12 oz Ham (deli slices, chopped)
- 2 cups fat-free shredded mozzarella cheese (divided)

Preparation

1. Preheat the oven to 450 degrees F
2. In a large bowl, toss the cauliflower with oil. Season with sea salt and black pepper.
3. Arrange the cauliflower on a baking sheet. Roast in the oven for about 30 minutes, until golden on the edges.
4. Meanwhile, in a large bowl, stir together Greek yogurt with corn starch, additional yogurt, Dijon mustard, minced garlic, and half of the shredded cheese (1 cup). Stir in the chicken and ham.
5. When the cauliflower is done, take it out of the oven and reduce the oven temperature to 400 degrees F. Stir the cauliflower into the bowl.
6. Transfer the casserole mixture into a casserole dish. Top with remaining shredded Swiss cheese. Bake for 10 minutes, until the cheese is melted and golden, and the casserole is bubbly.
7. If desired, sprinkle crushed pork rinds on top for a bread-crumb-like effect or garnish with fresh chives.

Chicken Chili

By Christine Maier

Makes 12 Servings

Ingredients

- 18 oz cooked boneless skinless chicken breast - chopped or shredded
- 1 jar Herdez Salsa
- 1 can great northern beans
- 1 can Rotel tomatoes
- 1 bag riced cauliflower
- 1 cup frozen onion and bell peppers
- 8 oz ⅓ fat cream cheese
- 3 cups chicken broth
- 2 tsp ground cumin
- 1 tsp onion powder

Preparation

1. Combine all ingredients except cream cheese into a big stew pot and let simmer for 15 - 20 minutes.
2. Add cream cheese and blend. Serve immediately.

Chicken Chilli (Christine Maier)

Nutrition Facts

Serving Size: 1 Serving

Amount Per Serving		% Daily Value*
Calories	159.7 kcal	8 %
Total Fat	5.3 g	8 %
Saturated Fat	3.1 g	15 %
Trans Fat	0 g	
Cholesterol	58.7 mg	20 %
Sodium	664.2 mg	28 %
Total Carbohydrate	9 g	3 %
Dietary Fiber	2.6 g	10 %
Sugars	2.7 g	
Protein	16.8 g	34 %
Vitamin A	4 % • Vitamin C	2 %
Calcium	5 % • Iron	8 %

* Percent Daily Values are based on a 2,000 calorie diet. Your daily values may be higher or lower depending on your calorie needs.

Full Info at cronometer.com

Chicken and Veggie Pan Meal

By Lindsey Barak

Makes 4 Servings

Ingredients

- 4 medium boneless, skinless chicken breasts
- 3 cups chopped raw broccoli
- 3 cups chopped raw cauliflower
- 1 tbsp olive oil
- Seasoning of choice

Preparation

1. Cut chicken into small tenders.
2. Toss all ingredients with seasoning of choice and lay out on a sheet pan.
3. Bake at 350 for approximately 30 minutes. Check chicken for doneness.

Chicken & Veggy Pan Meal (Lindsey Barak)

Nutrition Facts

Serving Size: 1 Serving

Amount Per Serving		% Daily Value*
Calories	299.8 kcal	15 %
Total Fat	9.7 g	15 %
Saturated Fat	2.1 g	11 %
Trans Fat	0.1 g	
Cholesterol	102 mg	34 %
Sodium	154.4 mg	6 %
Total Carbohydrate	12.2 g	4 %
Dietary Fiber	6 g	24 %
Sugars	3.6 g	
Protein	41.6 g	83 %
Vitamin A	37 % • Vitamin C	195 %
Calcium	8 % • Iron	13 %

* Percent Daily Values are based on a 2,000 calorie diet. Your daily values may be higher or lower depending on your calorie needs.

Full Info at cronometer.com </>

Buffalo Chicken Casserole

By Julie Houston

Buffalo Chicken Casserole (Julie Houston)

Nutrition Facts
Serving Size: 1 Serving

Amount Per Serving		% Daily Value*
Calories	175.7 kcal	9 %
Total Fat	4 g	6 %
Saturated Fat	2.2 g	11 %
Trans Fat	0.1 g	
Cholesterol	31.1 mg	10 %
Sodium	502.1 mg	21 %
Total Carbohydrate	12.9 g	4 %
Dietary Fiber	2.8 g	11 %
Sugars	5.6 g	
Protein	23.2 g	46 %
Vitamin A	13 % • Vitamin C	69 %
Calcium	35 % • Iron	3 %

* Percent Daily Values are based on a 2,000 calorie diet. Your daily values may be higher or lower depending on your calorie needs.

Full Info at cronometer.com </>

Makes 8 Servings

Ingredients

- 2 1/2 cups cooked shredded Chicken
- 1 cup bell pepper (red, orange, yellow)
- 1 tbsp garlic
- 2 cups yellow onion
- 1/4 cup hot sauce
- Salt and pepper
- 1 tbsp olive oil
- 2 Tbsp butter
- 2 1/4 cups fat-free cheddar cheese
- 3/4 cup non-fat Greek yogurt
- 2 cups carrot/broccoli slaw
- 1 bag riced cauliflower, thawed

Preparation

1. Add olive oil to a pan over medium high heat. Add in onion and cook for about five minutes, stirring occasionally so it doesn't burn. Add in carrot/broccoli slaw, bell pepper and garlic, cook for another three minutes or until soft.

2. In a baking dish, add the melted butter, hot sauce, and Greek yogurt. Mix together well. Then add in shredded chicken. Coat chicken in yogurt/hot sauce mixture.

3. Add in onion, slaw, bell pepper mixture. Combine well. Add riced cauliflower and combine well again. Add in half of the cheese, combine well. Top with remaining cheese.

4. Cook at 375 for 15 minutes until cheese is bubbly on top. You can also broil for about 5 minutes if you'd like.

Beef and Veggie Soup

By Christine Maier

Makes 10 Servings

Ingredients

- 32 oz. ground venison OR 97% lean ground beef
- 8 oz raw chopped celery
- ½ large yellow onion chopped
- 4 cups beef broth
- 3 cups diced baby red potatoes
- 4 oz chopped carrots
- 8 oz green beans
- 1 can petite diced tomatoes
- 1 6 oz can tomato paste
- 3 tbsp minced garlic
- 1 tsp onion powder
- 1 tsp thyme
- 1 tsp oregano
- Salt and pepper to taste

Preparation

1. Brown ground beef with onion and celery in a big stew pot.

2. Add remaining ingredients and simmer for about 30 minutes or until the veggies are tender.

Beef and Veggie Soup (Christine Maier)

Nutrition Facts

Serving Size: 1 Serving

Amount Per Serving		% Daily Value*
Calories	226.7 kcal	11 %
Total Fat	6.3 g	10 %
Saturated Fat	3 g	15 %
Trans Fat	0.2 g	
Cholesterol	74.1 mg	25 %
Sodium	311.6 mg	13 %
Total Carbohydrate	19 g	6 %
Dietary Fiber	3.9 g	16 %
Sugars	5 g	
Protein	22.9 g	46 %
Vitamin A	12 % • Vitamin C	24 %
Calcium	5 % • Iron	23 %

* Percent Daily Values are based on a 2,000 calorie diet. Your daily values may be higher or lower depending on your calorie needs.

Full Info at cronometer.com

Beef and Broccoli Stir Fry

By Jackie Schwartz

Makes 4 Servings

Ingredients

- 16 oz beef top round cut in strips
- 2 cloves garlic, minced
- 1 ½ cups onion, chopped
- 2 tbsp olive oil
- 1 bunch of broccoli
- 6 tbsp soy sauce
- 3 tbsp cornstarch
- 2 tbsp brown sugar

Preparation

1. Cook onion, garlic and Beef (cut in strips) in olive oil. When beef is rare add broccoli.
2. Mix soy sauce, cornstarch and brown sugar together in small bowl.
3. When broccoli is tender crisp pour sauce in pan and stir until just thickened.

Beef and Broccoli Stir Fry

Nutrition Facts

Serving Size: 1 Serving

Amount Per Serving		% Daily Value*
Calories	376.5 kcal	19 %
Total Fat	12.6 g	19 %
Saturated Fat	3 g	15 %
Trans Fat	0.3 g	
Cholesterol	87.3 mg	29 %
Sodium	1443.9 mg	60 %
Total Carbohydrate	28.3 g	9 %
Dietary Fiber	5.2 g	21 %
Sugars	10.2 g	
Protein	41 g	82 %
Vitamin A	19 % • Vitamin C	236 %
Calcium	12 % • Iron	28 %

* Percent Daily Values are based on a 2,000 calorie diet. Your daily values may be higher or lower depending on your calorie needs.

Full Info at cronometer.com   </>

Cabbage Stew

By Jackie Schwartz

Makes 6 Servings

Ingredients

- 16oz 93% Lean Ground Turkey
- 2 cups Diced Onions
- 2 14.5oz cans Petite Diced Tomatoes
- 2 14.5oz cans Red Kidney Beans
- 6 cups Chopped Cabbage
- 1 tbsp Chili Powder
- 1 tbsp Salt

Preparation

1. Brown turkey and onion in a big pot.
2. Add all remaining ingredients and let simmer until cabbage is tender.
3. Add water if a thinner soup is preferred and adjust salt and chili powder to taste.

Cabbage Stew 2

Nutrition Facts

Serving Size: 1 Serving

Amount Per Serving		% Daily Value*
Calories	364.6 kcal	18 %
Total Fat	9.7 g	15 %
Saturated Fat	2.4 g	12 %
Trans Fat	0.1 g	
Cholesterol	78.6 mg	26 %
Sodium	1665.4 mg	69 %
Total Carbohydrate	38.7 g	13 %
Dietary Fiber	12.2 g	49 %
Sugars	9.8 g	
Protein	31.9 g	64 %
Vitamin A	11 % • Vitamin C	62 %
Calcium	14 % • Iron	26 %

* Percent Daily Values are based on a 2,000 calorie diet. Your daily values may be higher or lower depending on your calorie needs.

Full Info at cronometer.com

Cajun Stir Fry

By Jackie Schwartz

Makes 4 Servings

Ingredients

- 16oz 93% Lean Ground Beef
- 4 Medium Zucchini, Raw
- 2 cups Frozen Onion and Bell Pepper Blend
- 2 Cloves Garlic, Diced
- 2 Tsp Old Bay Seasoning Mix

Preparation

1. Dice or slice zucchini and mushrooms.
2. Saute garlic, onion/pepper blend and ground beef.
3. When meat is cooked, add zucchini and mushrooms.
4. Season with Old Bay seasoning.

Cajun Stir fry

Nutrition Facts

Serving Size: 1 Serving

Amount Per Serving		% Daily Value*
Calories	290.8 kcal	15 %
Total Fat	10.6 g	16 %
Saturated Fat	4.2 g	21 %
Trans Fat	0.3 g	
Cholesterol	99.8 mg	33 %
Sodium	413.5 mg	17 %
Total Carbohydrate	12.8 g	4 %
Dietary Fiber	3.6 g	15 %
Sugars	8.7 g	
Protein	37.1 g	74 %
Vitamin A	10 % • Vitamin C	76 %
Calcium	5 % • Iron	26 %

*Percent Daily Values are based on a 2,000 calorie diet. Your daily values may be higher or lower depending on your calorie needs.

Full info at cronometer.com </>

Tip

*Serve with Red Devil hot sauce.
**Ground turkey, chicken, pork or turkey sausage can be substituted for ground beef.
***Change the Flavor - substitute Taco Season for Old Bay and serve with Salsa and a spoonful of Greek yogurt

Chicken Bacon Ranch Casserole

By Julie Houston

Makes 8 Servings

Ingredients

- 32 oz cooked boneless skinless chicken breast, shredded or chopped
- 8 slices of turkey bacon cooked and chopped
- 2 tsp minced garlic
- ¾ cup Walden Farms Calorie Free Ranch Dressing
- 4 cups frozen chopped spinach, drained
- 1 cup fat free shredded cheddar cheese
- 1 cup fat free shredded mozzarella cheese

Preparation

1. Mix ½ of the cheddar and mozzarella cheese with all the remaining ingredients.
2. Put into a sprayed casserole dish. Top with remaining cheese.
3. Bake at 350 degrees for about 20 minutes.

Chicken Bacon Ranch Casserole (Julie Houston)

Nutrition Facts

Serving Size: 1 Serving

Amount Per Serving		% Daily Value*
Calories	215.5 kcal	11 %
Total Fat	5 g	8 %
Saturated Fat	1.5 g	8 %
Trans Fat	0 g	
Cholesterol	72.7 mg	24 %
Sodium	557.7 mg	23 %
Total Carbohydrate	3.5 g	1 %
Dietary Fiber	0.5 g	2 %
Sugars	0.8 g	
Protein	37.1 g	74 %
Vitamin A	9 % • Vitamin C	0 %
Calcium	30 % • Iron	3 %

* Percent Daily Values are based on a 2,000 calorie diet. Your daily values may be higher or lower depending on your calorie needs.

Full Info at cronometer.com `</>`

Tip

This is great on top of cauliflower rice or quinoa.

Chicken Verde

By Jackie Schwartz

Makes 8 Servings

Ingredients

- 1 15.7oz bottle of Herdez Salsa Verde
- 1.5 cups Frozen Chopped Onion
- 3 Chopped Cloves of Garlic
- 1 Package Taco Seasoning Mix
- 2 pounds Boneless Skinless Chicken Breasts

Preparation

1. Put all ingredients into a crockpot.
2. Cook on low for 6 to 8 hours.

Chicken Verde

Nutrition Facts

Serving Size: 1 Serving

Amount Per Serving		% Daily Value*
Calories	232.1 kcal	12 %
Total Fat	5.1 g	8 %
Saturated Fat	1.4 g	7 %
Trans Fat	0.1 g	
Cholesterol	96.4 mg	32 %
Sodium	729 mg	30 %
Total Carbohydrate	7.5 g	2 %
Dietary Fiber	0.3 g	1 %
Sugars	2.8 g	
Protein	35.1 g	70 %
Vitamin A	1 % • Vitamin C	8 %
Calcium	2 % • Iron	8 %

* Percent Daily Values are based on a 2,000 calorie diet. Your daily values may be higher or lower depending on your calorie needs.

Full Info at cronometer.com </>

Tip

This makes a great filling for tacos, burritos, taco bowls and taco salad.

Chicken Taco Soup

By Jackie Schwartz

Makes 4 Servings

Ingredients
- 1 12 oz can of chicken breast
- 1 can of black bean
- 1 can of hominy
- 1- 24oz jar of salsa
- 1 package of taco seasoning

Preparation
1. Empty cans of chicken, beans, and hominy into a pot and add a jar of salsa. Add some taco season if preferred. Warm up on the stove or in the microwave.
2. Can be topped with Greek yogurt, low-fat sour cream, low fat cheese and a little avocado.

Chicken Taco Soup

Nutrition Facts

Serving Size: 1 Serving

Amount Per Serving		% Daily Value*
Calories	273.9 kcal	14 %
Total Fat	3.2 g	5 %
Saturated Fat	0.1 g	0 %
Trans Fat	0 g	
Cholesterol	45 mg	15 %
Sodium	2934.1 mg	122 %
Total Carbohydrate	41.2 g	14 %
Dietary Fiber	9.6 g	38 %
Sugars	8.8 g	
Protein	19.7 g	39 %
Vitamin A	14 % • Vitamin C	0 %
Calcium	5 % • Iron	16 %

* Percent Daily Values are based on a 2,000 calorie diet. Your daily values may be higher or lower depending on your calorie needs.

Full Info at cronometer.com </>

Tip

I keep these cans of ingredients in the pantry as a staple when we need a last-minute meal!

Coconut Curry Chicken

By Jackie Schwartz

Makes 4 Servings

Ingredients

- 32 oz boneless skinless chicken thighs
- 2 cloves garlic, minced
- 32 oz frozen broccoli florets
- 1 can of coconut milk
- 1 oz of white wine
- 2 tbsp cornstarch
- Curry powder
- Salt and pepper to taste

Preparation

1. Cube chicken and brown with garlic. Add Broccoli and saute until almost done.
2. Mix coconut milk with wine and cornstarch. Add to the skillet and thicken.
3. Add curry powder and salt to taste

Coconut Curry Chicken

Nutrition Facts

Serving Size: 1 Serving

Amount Per Serving		% Daily Value*
Calories	469.2 kcal	23 %
Total Fat	24.4 g	38 %
Saturated Fat	7.5 g	38 %
Trans Fat	0 g	
Cholesterol	182.2 mg	61 %
Sodium	395.1 mg	17 %
Total Carbohydrate	19.3 g	6 %
Dietary Fiber	6.1 g	24 %
Sugars	5.9 g	
Protein	39.4 g	79 %
Vitamin A	0 % • Vitamin C	130 %
Calcium	6 % • Iron	14 %

* Percent Daily Values are based on a 2,000 calorie diet. Your daily values may be higher or lower depending on your calorie needs.

Full Info at cronometer.com   </>

Tip

Traditionally served over rice. If you have the calories in your budget eat it over rice with your kids, if not, eat it over cauliflower rice.

Creamy Cajun Pasta

By Jackie Schwartz

Makes 5 Servings

Ingredients

- 2 10oz bags of frozen zucchini lentil pasta
- 1 20oz bag of frozen onion and bell pepper blend
- 16 oz mushrooms
- 2 15oz cans of diced tomatoes
- 3 tbsp diced garlic
- 13oz Turkey Kielbasa
- 1 cup non fat greek yogurt
- Cajun Seasoning to taste

Preparation

1. Brown onion bell pepper mix and mushrooms with garlic.
2. Chop Kielbasa and add with tomatoes and pasta until warm.
3. Add yogurt and cajun season to taste.

Creamy Cajun Pasta

Nutrition Facts

Serving Size: 1 Serving

Amount Per Serving		% Daily Value*
Calories	381.5 kcal	19 %
Total Fat	10.9 g	17 %
Saturated Fat	2.6 g	13 %
Trans Fat	0 g	
Cholesterol	58.1 mg	19 %
Sodium	1185.7 mg	49 %
Total Carbohydrate	39.9 g	13 %
Dietary Fiber	5.8 g	23 %
Sugars	14.3 g	
Protein	29.7 g	59 %
Vitamin A	18 % • Vitamin C	46 %
Calcium	20 % • Iron	24 %

* Percent Daily Values are based on a 2,000 calorie diet. Your daily values may be higher or lower depending on your calorie needs.

Full Info at cronometer.com </>

Eggroll in a Bowl

By Jackie Schwartz

Makes 4 Servings

Ingredients

- 16oz 93% lean ground turkey
- 1 tbsp sesame oil
- 1 cup chopped onions
- 2 cloves garlic, minced
- 2 tsp ginger paste
- 1 16 oz bag of cole slaw cabbage
- ¼ cup soy sauce

Preparation

1. Sauté onion in sesame oil. Add ground turkey and garlic and ginger. Cook until brown.
2. Add Cole Slaw mix and Soy sauce and sauté until desired tenderness.
3. Can be served with brown rice or Quinoa.

Egg Roll in a Bowl

Nutrition Facts

Serving Size: 1 Serving

Amount Per Serving		% Daily Value*
Calories	254.9 kcal	13 %
Total Fat	13.9 g	21 %
Saturated Fat	3 g	15 %
Trans Fat	0.1 g	
Cholesterol	85.1 mg	28 %
Sodium	1001.3 mg	42 %
Total Carbohydrate	10 g	3 %
Dietary Fiber	3.3 g	13 %
Sugars	5.1 g	
Protein	24.2 g	48 %
Vitamin A	22 % • Vitamin C	68 %
Calcium	9 % • Iron	12 %

* Percent Daily Values are based on a 2,000 calorie diet. Your daily values may be higher or lower depending on your calorie needs.

Full Info at cronometer.com

Ginger "Honey" Pork

By Jackie Schwartz

Makes 4 Servings

Ingredients
- ¼ cup Soy Sauce
- ½ cup Swerve Brown Sugar Replacement
- 2 tbsp chopped Garlic
- 1.5 tsp raw Ginger Root
- 2 tsp Onion Powder
- 4 tbsp Sugar Free Maple Pancake Syrup
- 3 tbsp Cornstarch
- 1 cup Tap Water
- 16oz Center Loin Pork Chops
- 8oz raw Snow Peas
- 3 large Red Bell Peppers
- 1 crown Broccoli

Preparation
1. Mix first 8 ingredients in small saucepan to thicken.
2. Cut pork and bell pepper into strips. Cut broccoli into florets.
3. Put pork and veggies into a gallon Ziplock and toss with sauce.
4. Spread on sheet pan and bake at 350 for about 30 minutes.

Ginger "Honey" Pork

Nutrition Facts

Serving Size: 1 Serving

Amount Per Serving		% Daily Value*
Calories	351.3 kcal	18 %
Total Fat	7.5 g	11 %
Saturated Fat	2.3 g	12 %
Trans Fat	0 g	
Cholesterol	86.2 mg	29 %
Sodium	1035.7 mg	43 %
Total Carbohydrate	57.6 g	19 %
Dietary Fiber	8.5 g	34 %
Sugars	10.2 g	
Protein	40.8 g	82 %
Vitamin A	108 % • Vitamin C	547 %
Calcium	14 % • Iron	23 %

* Percent Daily Values are based on a 2,000 calorie diet. Your daily values may be higher or lower depending on your calorie needs.

Full Info at cronometer.com

Italian Zucchini Noodles

By Jackie Schwartz

Makes 4 Servings

Ingredients

- 8 oz frozen seasoning blend
- 8 oz mushrooms
- 9 oz canned artichoke hearts
- 3 medium zucchini
- 1 tbsp olive oil
- 16 oz turkey breakfast sausage
- 3 cloves garlic, minced
- 1 tbsp Italian seasoning
- ½ cup Greek yogurt

Preparation

1. Spin zucchini in a noodle maker.
2. Cook sausage with onion/pepper blend and garlic. Add mushrooms and cook down a few minutes. Add Zucchini noodles and Italian seasoning. Add artichoke hearts. Cook until noodles reach desired consistency. Add yogurt.

Italian Zucchini and Sausage Noodles

Nutrition Facts

Serving Size: 1 Serving

Amount Per Serving		% Daily Value*
Calories	362 kcal	18 %
Total Fat	14.4 g	22 %
Saturated Fat	3.7 g	19 %
Trans Fat	0 g	
Cholesterol	121.4 mg	40 %
Sodium	992.3 mg	41 %
Total Carbohydrate	21.9 g	7 %
Dietary Fiber	6.7 g	27 %
Sugars	10.6 g	
Protein	35.4 g	71 %
Vitamin A	7 % • Vitamin C	57 %
Calcium	14 % • Iron	22 %

*Percent Daily Values are based on a 2,000 calorie diet. Your daily values may be higher or lower depending on your calorie needs.

Full Info at cronometer.com

One Pan Oven Pork Chops

By Jackie Schwartz

Makes 4 Servings

Ingredients

- 16 oz pork chops
- 3 cups chopped potatoes
- 4 cups green beans
- 3 tsp olive oil
- 2 packets Lipton Onion Soup Mix

Preparation

1. In a one-gallon Ziplock bag add pork chops, one teaspoon olive oil and one soup mix packet. Shake well and let brine for 30 minutes to an hour if possible.
2. In another gallon Ziplock add chopped potatoes and green beans, 2 teaspoons olive oil and a second packet of onion soup mix.
3. Dump vegetables and pork chops on a sheet pan and put in the oven at 350 for 35 minutes. Check the doneness of pork before removing. Pork may finish and need to rest before vegetables are tender.

Oven Pork Chops, Potatoes and green beans

Nutrition Facts

Serving Size: 1 Serving

Amount Per Serving		% Daily Value*
Calories	428.6 kcal	21 %
Total Fat	15.2 g	23 %
Saturated Fat	4.6 g	23 %
Trans Fat	0 g	
Cholesterol	94.1 mg	31 %
Sodium	1291.9 mg	54 %
Total Carbohydrate	34.3 g	11 %
Dietary Fiber	6.7 g	27 %
Sugars	6.3 g	
Protein	36.8 g	74 %
Vitamin A	14 % • Vitamin C	36 %
Calcium	6 % • Iron	18 %

* Percent Daily Values are based on a 2,000 calorie diet. Your daily values may be higher or lower depending on your calorie needs.

Full Info at cronometer.com

Sauerkraut Skillet

By Jackie Schwartz

Makes 3 Servings

Ingredients

- 4 cups frozen onion bell pepper blend
- 2 cloves garlic, minced
- 4 cups German Style Sauerkraut
- 13oz turkey kielbasa

Preparation

1. Sauté onion and pepper mixture with garlic.
2. Slice Kielbasa and add to skillet. Add jar of sauerkraut. Season with salt, pepper, caraway seed and no calorie sweetener (if you like)

Sauerkraut Skillet

Nutrition Facts

Serving Size: 1 Serving

Amount Per Serving		% Daily Value*
Calories	271.3 kcal	14 %
Total Fat	13 g	20 %
Saturated Fat	3.3 g	16 %
Trans Fat	0 g	
Cholesterol	75.8 mg	25 %
Sodium	2345.3 mg	98 %
Total Carbohydrate	31.5 g	10 %
Dietary Fiber	9.9 g	40 %
Sugars	11.7 g	
Protein	22.5 g	45 %
Vitamin A	0 % • Vitamin C	1 %
Calcium	19 % • Iron	14 %

* Percent Daily Values are based on a 2,000 calorie diet. Your daily values may be higher or lower depending on your calorie needs.

Full Info at cronometer.com </>

Zucchini Lasagna

By Jackie Schwartz

Makes 6 Servings

Ingredients

- 3 medium zucchinis
- 1 ½ cups frozen onion and pepper blend
- 3 cloves garlic, minced
- 16 oz turkey breakfast sausage
- 16 oz mushrooms, sliced
- 4 ½ cups pasta sauce
- 1 cup part skim ricotta cheese
- 1 cup 1% cottage cheese
- 2 cups mozzarella cheese
- ½ cup parmesan cheese
- 4 large egg whites

Preparation

1. Slice Zucchini in a planer and roast in the oven until tender.
2. Cook Onion/pepper blend with garlic and sausage. Add mushrooms and brown. Add Pasta sauce and Italian Season.
3. In separate bowl mix egg whites, Parmesan cheese, ricotta cheese, cottage cheese, and 1.5 cups Mozzarella cheese.
4. Layer Zucchini lasagna noodles in a pan with sauce and cheese like regular lasagna. Bake at 350 for about 35 minutes. Top with 1/2 cup Mozzarella cheese and bake for 10 more minutes.

Zucchini Lasagne

Nutrition Facts

Serving Size: 1 Serving

Amount Per Serving		% Daily Value*
Calories	447.8 kcal	22 %
Total Fat	20.5 g	31 %
Saturated Fat	9.8 g	49 %
Trans Fat	0.2 g	
Cholesterol	73.5 mg	24 %
Sodium	1597.6 mg	67 %
Total Carbohydrate	24.4 g	8 %
Dietary Fiber	4.6 g	18 %
Sugars	12.1 g	
Protein	42.1 g	84 %
Vitamin A	21 % • Vitamin C	49 %
Calcium	53 % • Iron	17 %

* Percent Daily Values are based on a 2,000 calorie diet. Your daily values may be higher or lower depending on your calorie needs.

Full Info at cronometer.com </>

Zucchini Tacos

By Gris Perez

Makes 4 Servings

Ingredients

- 8 Medium zucchinis
- 8 oz. 93% Lean ground beef
- 1 cup chopped red bell pepper
- 1 cup chopped yellow bell pepper
- 2 tsp ground cumin
- 2 tsp paprika
- 2 tsp garlic powder
- Salt
- 2 cups grated fat free mozzarella cheese

Preparation

1. Sauté bell peppers with ground beef and spiced.
2. Cut zucchini in half and spoon out the middle to make a boat. Fill with cooked ground beef mix and top with shredded cheese.
3. Bake in oven at 350 until zucchini are tender - about 20 minutes.

Zucchini Tacos

Nutrition Facts

Serving Size: 1 Serving

Amount Per Serving		% Daily Value*
Calories	269 kcal	13 %
Total Fat	6 g	9 %
Saturated Fat	2 g	10 %
Trans Fat	0 g	
Cholesterol	42.7 mg	14 %
Sodium	835.5 mg	35 %
Total Carbohydrate	20.7 g	7 %
Dietary Fiber	5.7 g	23 %
Sugars	15.3 g	
Protein	35.7 g	71 %
Vitamin A	70 % • Vitamin C	282 %
Calcium	59 % • Iron	23 %

* Percent Daily Values are based on a 2,000 calorie diet. Your daily values may be higher or lower depending on your calorie needs.

Full Info at cronometer.com   </>

Desserts

"Apple Crisp"

By Amanda Ford

Makes 9 Servings

Ingredients

- 4 cups chopped zucchini
- ½ cup lemon juice
- 2 tbsp butter
- ½ cup golden monk fruit
- ½ tsp xanthan gum
- 2 tsp cinnamon
- 1 tsp nutmeg
- 1 stick butter
- 1 cup chopped pecans
- ½ cup golden monk fruit
- 1 cup almond flour
- 1 tsp cinnamon

Preparation

1. Preheat the oven to 350°
2. Peel and cut the zucchini. If the zucchini is on the larger side, then make sure to take out some of the seeds.
3. In a Dutch oven, turn heat on medium-high and add the butter. Once butter is melted let it start to brown, but don't burn it. Now that the butter is browned add the zucchini to the pan.
4. Add cinnamon, nutmeg, and monk fruit to the zucchini and stir well. Then pour in lemon juice and add xanthan gum.
5. Cook on medium heat for at least 20 minutes. Keep stirring mixture to make sure it doesn't stick to the bottom of the pan.
6. In a small, separate bowl combine the softened butter, chopped pecans, almond flour, and cinnamon together. To really mix it in well, you might need to use your hands.
7. Once the zucchini is cooked, transfer it to an 8"x8" baking dish. Sprinkle the topping over the squash, you should have enough to completely cover it.
8. Bake in the oven for about 30 minutes or until the top is crispy and the fruit is bubbling.

Pumpkin Bread Pudding

By Jackie Schwartz

Makes 4 Servings

Ingredients
- 9 slices Aldi Zero Net Carb bread
- 1 can Pumpkin Puree
- 2 large eggs
- 1 ½ cups almond milk
- 1 cup Swerve Granular Sugar Replacement
- 1 scoop Vanilla MyProtein powder
- 1 tsp salt
- 2 tsp cinnamon
- 2 tsp pumpkin pie spice

Preparation
1. Tear or cut bread into small cubes and place in a 9x11 casserole dish.
2. Mix all remaining ingredients and pour over bread. Let soak for at least an hour.
3. Bake in oven at 350 degrees for an hour or until set in the middle.

Pumpkin bread pudding

Nutrition Facts

Serving Size: 1 Serving

Amount Per Serving		% Daily Value*
Calories	208.8 kcal	10 %
Total Fat	6.7 g	10 %
Saturated Fat	1.1 g	5 %
Trans Fat	0 g	
Cholesterol	108.3 mg	36 %
Sodium	300.3 mg	13 %
Total Carbohydrate	78.6 g	26 %
Dietary Fiber	23.1 g	92 %
Sugars	4.9 g	
Protein	20.1 g	40 %
Vitamin A	225 % • Vitamin C	4 %
Calcium	28 % • Iron	8 %

* Percent Daily Values are based on a 2,000 calorie diet. Your daily values may be higher or lower depending on your calorie needs.

Full Info at cronometer.com   </>

Tip

Can be drizzled with sugar free syrup or icing made with Splenda, almond milk and vanilla.

Banana Bread

By Julie Houston

Makes 24 Servings

Ingredients

- 4 medium bananas
- 1 ½ cups almond flour
- 12 grams granulated Stevia
- 2 tsp baking soda
- ½ tsp salt
- ⅔ cup egg whites
- ½ cup unsweetened applesauce
- 4 tsp vanilla extract
- 2 cups fat free Greek yogurt
- 1 ½ cups vanilla or cinnamon flavored protein powder

Preparation

1. Preheat oven to 375
2. Grease 2 loaf pans with coconut oil and line with parchment paper.
3. In a bowl, mash bananas first until smooth, then add rest of ingredients, mix until well blended
4. Pour ingredients into pans and bake for approximately 25 minutes and check with a toothpick

Protein Banana Bread (Julie Houston)

Nutrition Facts

Serving Size: 1 Serving

Amount Per Serving		% Daily Value*
Calories	106 kcal	5 %
Total Fat	4 g	6 %
Saturated Fat	0.5 g	3 %
Trans Fat	0 g	
Cholesterol	5.2 mg	2 %
Sodium	127.3 mg	5 %
Total Carbohydrate	9.1 g	3 %
Dietary Fiber	1.6 g	6 %
Sugars	5.1 g	
Protein	8.7 g	17 %
Vitamin A	0 % • Vitamin C	3 %
Calcium	5 % • Iron	2 %

* Percent Daily Values are based on a 2,000 calorie diet. Your daily values may be higher or lower depending on your calorie needs.

Full Info at cronometer.com </>

Low Fat Cupcakes

By Jackie Schwartz

Makes 24 Servings

Ingredients

- 1 box cake mix of choice
- 1 can pumpkin puree
- 4 large egg whites

Preparation

1. Mix all ingredients pour into 24 cupcake liners.
2. Bake at 350 degrees for about 20 minutes.

Low-fat Cupcakes

Nutrition Facts

Serving Size: 1 Serving

Amount Per Serving		% Daily Value*
Calories	81 kcal	4 %
Total Fat	1.7 g	3 %
Saturated Fat	0 g	0 %
Trans Fat	0 g	
Cholesterol	0 mg	0 %
Sodium	10 mg	0 %
Total Carbohydrate	15.2 g	5 %
Dietary Fiber	0.9 g	3 %
Sugars	7.9 g	
Protein	1.6 g	3 %
Vitamin A	36 % • Vitamin C	1 %
Calcium	0 % • Iron	1 %

* Percent Daily Values are based on a 2,000 calorie diet. Your daily values may be higher or lower depending on your calorie needs.

Full Info at cronometer.com   </>

Tip:

Can be made with Chocolate, Spice or Carrot cake mix - all are yummy!

Protein "Ice Cream"

By Jackie Schwartz

Makes 1 Serving

Ingredients

- 1 ½ cups ice
- 1 packet stevia
- ½ tbsp xanthan gum
- ½ oz sugar free flavored syrup
- 1 scoop protein powder
- 1 cup almond milk
- 6 tsp oat fiber

Preparation

1. Mix all ingredients in a Blender and serve.

Protein Ice Cream

Nutrition Facts

Serving Size: 1 full recipe — 469g

Amount Per Serving		% Daily Value*
Calories	158.6 kcal	8 %
Total Fat	4.5 g	7 %
Saturated Fat	0.7 g	3 %
Trans Fat	0 g	
Cholesterol	55 mg	18 %
Sodium	354.3 mg	15 %
Total Carbohydrate	23.5 g	8 %
Dietary Fiber	25.1 g	101 %
Sugars	3.1 g	
Protein	19.6 g	39 %
Vitamin A	11 % • Vitamin C	0 %
Calcium	57 % • Iron	4 %

* Percent Daily Values are based on a 2,000 calorie diet. Your daily values may be higher or lower depending on your calorie needs.

Full Info a: cronometer.com   </>

Tip

By using different flavors of protein powder and syrup the possibilities are almost endless. Xanthan gum is a thickener which will turn your shake to the consistency of soft serve ice cream. Be careful - it can be sticky.

Afterword

OUR STORIES

Finding "ME" Again
(Jackie Schwartz)

I was never skinny as a kid. I wasn't fat but "solid" was often used to describe my build. In college, I loved the aerobics craze and worked out a lot. I found that my solid build was strong and I enjoyed lifting weights. I enjoyed it so much that I majored in Exercise Science. I looked great but not as good as the "skinny" girls around me - I was still more "solid". It was hard being a "thick" aerobics instructor—so hard that I turned to unhealthy practices and developed an eating disorder. I battled for a while with anorexia and bulimia, a cycle that wreaked havoc on my metabolism. After counseling, I vowed to take better care of my body, and healthy, nutritional food became important.

When I married, I weighed 145 pounds. I was in my BMI. I considered it my "happy weight", meaning I didn't kill myself working out. I just took a daily walk and ate healthy enough, still enjoying dinners out, wine and treats now and then. When I had my kids, I was able to return to, and maintain, that 145 pound "happy weight". As I neared 40, several things happened. My hormones started to change. Weight crept on, slowly at first. My marriage was deteriorating. I wasn't paying attention to my weight or my health. I was too worried about everything else around me.

At 42, I could not save my marriage, and when I was forced to look at myself in pictures, I did not even recognize the person I saw anymore. I was embarrassed at how much weight I had put on. My weight had reached 185. Finding pictures at that weight is hard, because I avoided the camera like the plague. I avoided activities with my kids that involved shorts or a bathing suit. That summer, the doctor told me that my cholesterol was high and that I was borderline diabetic.

I knew I had to make changes—I was 40 pounds heavier than I was all of my adult life. And now I was single, and my boys were going to need me to BE THERE for them now more than ever. It was a traumatic time for them too, and I needed to be in a healthy place to support them. I knew how to eat healthy—I used to eat that way. I used to cook healthy family meals, not just rely on take out. I used to move more playing with the kids—not just veg out in front of the TV giving into depression. I felt guilty and realized what a bad example I had set for them the last few years. So, I took action.

I cleaned up my diet. I went back to eating "healthy enough", still enjoying dinners out, treats and wine. I also started walking again—nothing big, just a 25 to 30 minute walk about five days a week. The first summer at the doc was great. I had lost 20 pounds and the doc was happy. Moving from teaching in the classroom to teaching PE helped my activity level. But I got stuck at 150. I wanted so badly to be back at 145 and hear the doc say that I am in the healthy BMI range. I could not make it happen. I even joined a gym and started lifting weights again.

Then I met Jonas. At first, I gained a few pounds when we started dating. Dating was fun and we splurged a lot!! But it did not take long for me to decide I had to reign it back in. It was easy. I had a partner who had the same healthy goals in mind that I had. Jonas loved everything I cooked and was often shocked at the nutritional counts of our supper. He even enjoyed the healthy meals I packed for lunch so much that he asked me to prep some for him as well. I had hoped my weight-lifting workouts at the gym would get me to my goal, but it wasn't working. Jonas offered to create a program for me and be my coach. He told me he wanted me to give up my hour-long sessions several times a week for just 15 minutes a day.

I thought he was crazy. I wasn't sure I believed him when he told me that he only worked out 15 minutes a day. But I did it. And within weeks, I could see changes in my body. My muscles were suddenly responding to my workouts. I was getting stronger and at the same time getting leaner. While writing this, I now weigh 137 pounds. And last week my athlete son had to admit that I won our summer ab challenge.

I have no more issues doing activities with my children in a bathing suit. I can keep up with them, and my confidence is almost as high as my energy. I love knowing I am feeding my family quality food, still treating them (I LOVE to bake!) and showing them a healthy balance that they can carry on into their adult life. Being a parent isn't easy, knowing you are setting the foundation for your child's future is scary. The least I can do is try my best to set a healthy foundation!

—Jackie Nors Schwartz

Unlovable
(Jonas Schwartz)

I was a fat kid. Actually, in pretty much every class I was in through Junior High, I was THE fat kid. My granny raised me, and she fed me well—really well. She was loving her adopted son the best she knew how, but as my body grew fatter and fatter, I grew more and more miserable and isolated inside.

When I was 12 or 13, what I wanted most in the world was a girlfriend. I had a crush on a girl for years. But the last person any girl wanted was the fat nerd in school. I felt unlovable.

I remember sitting at home alone at night wishing I could take a knife and cut off my belly. I visualized the whole process. I would be free of that hateful burden. I would no longer be unlovable. Then someone could love me.

Puberty kicked in and I got a surge of motivation. I played volleyball, soccer, jogged and starved away a full 60 pounds by the time I was 15. That was amazing! I remember showing a friend on my volleyball team a photo of me when I was young and fat. He said, "Look! It's the kid who ate Schwartz!" LOL.

And then at age 35, I hit a wall. I had moved to Ennis Texas (south of Dallas) to take care of my Dad who had been diagnosed with ALS (Lou Gehrig's Disease). I moved in with him and my stepmom (who has gold, saint's wings waiting on her). I stayed home with him and helped however I could.

But, my magical youthful hormones had declined to aging levels, I couldn't devote hours to sports anymore, and I began putting weight back on. Within two years, I'd gained those 60 pounds back again, plus another 20.

I remember every time I would look in the mirror, I would think, "That's not ME." And I would hear my friend's voice in my ear saying, "Look, it's the guy who ate Schwartz!" I started feeling like I did when I was a young boy—alone and unlovable. Depression kicked in.

Around this time, my first grandson was born. I imagined all the wonderful things that we would be able to do together. I had not grown up living with my own father, so this was a chance to experience a side of life I had not personally known. I was going to make it count! I wanted him to know and love his Granddad.

Shortly after he was born, I remember sitting on my couch, putting on my shoes. Merely bending over to tie my laces turned into a traumatic event. I remember straining hard, all the blood rushing to my face, turning it bright red. When I was able to sit back up, my head was swimming. I was dizzy and seeing stars.

I don't know exactly what happened to me while trying to tie my shoes that day, but it was then I knew that my dreams of doing cool stuff with my new grandson were just silly fantasies. How was I going to teach him how to throw a football or how to ride a bike if I was in such bad shape that I couldn't even bend over to tie my shoes?

I knew, if I wanted to live much longer, if I wanted to play with my grandson, if I wanted him to actually know his granddad, I had to make my own health a priority in my life. One of the fathers of the church in a book called the Didache says there are two roads open before us, one leads to death, and one leads to life. I chose life.

I was older now, and I didn't have the energy I had as a kid, when I ran off that 60 pounds of baby fat. Plus, I had a job and a family. I couldn't give up hours out of my day to get this done. There were not enough hours in the day as it was. I knew I had work smarter, not harder. I had become a college professor, and so I did what I had been educated to do. I began researching.

If you've ever begun researching dieting and exercise, you know there is a ton of information out there, and one article conflicts with the next. There are a lot of "maps" on how to get out of those deep, dark woods of ill-health, but they say conflicting things. Logic says they can't ALL be right.

Luckily, I partnered with an enormously competent coach who did more than give me a map. He acted as my guide and got me out of those woods with scientifically verifiable principles tailored and applied to my particular situation. He filtered the signal from the noise, distilled the concepts into action steps, and showed me how to implement them within the parameters of my own particular personal life situation. That, my brothers and sisters, is priceless.

It took me a solid year of steady progress, but I lost the 60 pounds of fat and started gaining muscle. I'm not trying to win any powerlifting competitions, but having more muscle lets me eat more food and not get fat. And I like to eat! It really is the secret to fighting the hormonal decline as we age. I felt better. I had more energy. I had more confidence. I was treated differently. I saw ME in the mirror again, and for the first time, it was a positive, not a negative. At the time of this writing, I am 47 years old, and I am honestly in the best shape of my life—by far!

There is a reason for all the positive energy and emotion that comes with bodily health. Humans are not disembodied spirits. We are unities of body and soul. In my faith, our spirit is our intellect and identity, and our bodies are our channels of activity, as well as our very first gift from God. When either is sick, corrupt, or out of balance, we are not whole as we were made to be. And, I believe I will be called to account on how I cared for this fundamental gift. I want to hear, "Well done, my good and faithful servant. Since you were faithful in small matters, I will give you great responsibilities. Come, share your master's joy." (Mt 25:23).

I want that for other people too. If you can relate to that sad, lonely fat kid, or that aging man who no longer felt like "ME", then I want to help you. I now play with all my grandkids at the park and on the waterslides (yeah, I'm THAT guy), and you know what? I wouldn't trade that for the world. God bless you. Thanks for listening. Now, choose life.

—Jonas Schwartz

Philosophical & Ethical Justification for 15Minute.Fitness and Fit Families of Faith

I want to talk a little bit about the justification for our group, our program, and this book. Why Christian Moms and Dads—aren't all bodies the same? Of course. There is nothing unique about the biology of a Christian human body versus the human body of an atheist. But Christian parents are WHO we are, and therefore, they are our mission field.

"Mission Field" is the defining term, here. We see our coaching as a ministry—for health of the whole person—body and soul. My hero is St. Francis of Assisi. One of his quotes guides my life. He says, "Preach the Gospel at all times! And if necessary, use words."

The most powerful witness we will ever have is our lives—how we choose to live them. I want to model healthy behavior for those whom God has entrusted to my care. That is my cooperation with God's Providence. I want to help other Christian Moms and Dads model healthy behavior for their children.

If children saw more healthy role models, maybe then they might want to grow up to actually BE Christian Moms and Dads themselves. Instead, we see them more and more following the ways of modern society, which models broken families and faithlessness as the new "normal." We can fight this. We have to fight this. But, words are merely air tickling the ears. We must ACT. We must BE. We must model lives that our children respect and admire. This is how we "preach" most powerfully.

It could be argued that as Christians we are spiritual creatures, and therefore paying special attention to the body is ultimately counterproductive. I have heard this position. I understand it. And I am sympathetic to it. However, I do not share it. Here's why.

It is clear to me that the instant of my conception encompassed a two-fold gift—a brand new spirit was fused with a brand new body, neither of which had existed the moment before. Even taking into account the doctrine of original sin, it is certainly not the case that I was given a spirit by God and a body by Satan. No, God was the author of both, and what He gives is good.

It is not clear which one was given to me first. in fact, the most ancient Christian theological doctrine tells us that man is both spirit and flesh. True, St. Paul describes the internal moral conflict as a battle between the flesh and the spirit, but I think this points not toward some sort of fundamental evil nature of the body, but rather is an analogy to describe the seemingly impossible situation of being in conflict with oneself. After all, I am one single being. How can I be at odds with myself?

This is an ancient philosophical question (notably posed by Plato) which St. Paul picked up and examined theologically. I think using St. Paul's theological analogy as an excuse to ignore the health of the body is not defensible for the Christian. I am not a spirit who HAS a body. Neither am I a body which HAS a spirit. Rather, "I" am both, my body AND my spirit.

When I say "I" am hurt, I may be referring to either my spirit (emotional pain: sadness, heartbreak), or I may be referring to my body (physical pain: I stepped on a nail). Both my spirit and my body together make up WHAT I am as a human and WHO I am uniquely as an individual person. I do not exist and cannot function in the absence of either one of these two essential components of my being.

At the absolute least, I must admit that my body is my very first gift from God after I was brought into existence. If that is the case, do I not have a responsibility to care for, maintain, and provide for the flourishing of this primary gift from our heavenly father?

If your father gave you a new car, how do you think he would feel if you didn't take care of it? What if you neglected to change the oil or provide routine preventive maintenance? What if you fed it sewage instead of gasoline? What if you ignored it when the check engine light came on and continued to drive it without care, until it was rendered useless and was only worthy of the junkyard? Do you think your father would be very happy with you? Do you think this type of behavior shows respect and gratitude? Of course not.

I bet we can all agree that our bodies deserve at least as much care as our disposable vehicles. After all, we can't just go trade this body in on a new one at the year-end clearance sale. We're stuck with this one for the entirety of our life here on Earth. And when it ceases to work, we cease to live here.
With that in mind, I want to encourage you to begin this very day to look at your body in a new way. I hope you will look at it with gratitude. I hope you will look at it with a certain awe and holy fear. It is our very first gift from our Heavenly Father, and I want to help you make the most of your term of stewardship for this gift so that we may all here, "Well done good and faithful servant..."

And the best witness we can ever give to our children is to model healthy behavior. That includes spirit, mind AND body. God has shared his providential role in a special way with parents, who provide for the well-being of their children. Providing them with food, clothing and shelter takes care of their base survival needs right now, but that is a bare minimum.

Forming their habits and their character is the highest level of service we can render them, molding them into good people who will live happy lives after they leave our homes and lead families of their own. Let's be the role models they deserve.

Our Heavenly Father didn't just tell us what to do, He showed us what to do when He took on human flesh and guided us personally. Let's imitate Him and do the same for our children. Let's SHOW them how to be whole, happy and healthy, so that they can show their children, and they can in turn show their children. We can be the turning point in the history of our entire lineage. Think about that. Let this realization sink in. Let this opportunity excite you. Let it motivate you to become the person you were meant to be, fully alive and in healthy balance of spirit, mind, and body.

Blessings!

Moving Forward

If you bought a copy of this book, then I will give you 30 day access to my free beginner's workout program on the training app we use with our paid clients, "15minute.fitness". Just go to www.15minute.fitness and sign up for our "Free Foundations Course." It is a 1 page course with short videos that explains our basic approach. At the end of that page, you'll find the offer for free app access.

Too many people fail in their health and fitness pursuits due to lack of preparation. Taking the little time necessary to lay solid foundations makes all the difference. Our clients who have followed that 1 page course have shown exponentially better results than those who choose not to.

If you would like our ready-made 12 week course that walks you through this program one week at a time (both diet and weekly progressive workout routines), please check out our Premium program on www.15minute.fitness.

We also offer an Essentials (workouts-only) program which guides you through progressive 15 minute daily workouts. It insures you continue to provide the necessary level of stimulus required to keep your progress moving ever forward.

You have all the tools you need. All you have to do now is put it into practice! If you need further help implementing this, we're always here for you!

CONTACT US

Feel free to reach out to us. We'd love to hear from you!

www.15minute.fitness (website)
Fit Families of Faith (FB Group)
15 Minute Fitness (FB Page)
support@15minute.fitness (email)

ABOUT THE AUTHORS

Jackie completed her B.A. at the University of Texas at Arlington, where she double majored in Mathematics and Exercise Science. She has retired from teaching Mathematics & Physical Education to young people and now coaches adult clients full-time through *15Minute.Fitness,* the health and fitness coaching service they co-founded. She works toward a healthier, happier world, one family at a time.

Jonas is a professor of Philosophy, Ethics, History and Politics for Navarro College. He completed his PhD coursework at the University of Dallas, where he earned two of his three Masters degrees.

Jackie and Jonas live in a small town in North Texas. They enjoy their faith community, family time, camping, dancing and consuming the latest exercise and nutrition science research.

Made in the USA
Coppell, TX
11 October 2021

63745946R30066